THE FUTURE OF SEA POWER

IN THE PACIFIC

WORLD AFFAIRS PAMPHLETS

•

THE first aim of this series, published by the Foreign Policy Association and the World Peace Foundation, is to assist the citizen in understanding the forces underlying contemporary international problems, and acquaint him with the results of research in international relations. To this end, WORLD AFFAIRS PAMPHLETS are necessarily less detailed and more interpretative than the factual research data published by both organizations. The authors alone are responsible for any judgments or interpretations which may appear in this series; they will, however, be guided by the standards of objectivity and impartiality which characterize the *Foreign Policy Reports* and the *World Peace Foundation Publications*.

The second aim of the series is to secure a greater degree of cooperation between the various organizations dealing with foreign affairs. With this end in view, the publishers will consider meeting the request of any organization which desires the preparation of a pamphlet on a given subject in the international field.

WORLD AFFAIRS PAMPHLETS are sent regularly to members of the Foreign Policy Association and to subscribers of the World Peace Foundation.

March 1935

THE FUTURE OF SEA POWER IN THE PACIFIC

By

WALTER MILLIS

Author of

The Martial Spirit and *The Road to War*

PREPARED UNDER THE AUSPICES OF THE
AMERICAN COUNCIL, INSTITUTE OF PACIFIC RELATIONS

WORLD AFFAIRS PAMPHLETS No. 9

1935

Published jointly by

FOREIGN POLICY ASSOCIATION, NEW YORK
WORLD PEACE FOUNDATION, BOSTON

THE FUTURE OF SEA POWER IN THE PACIFIC

PRINTED IN THE UNITED STATES OF AMERICA
BY THE ACADEMY PRESS, NEW YORK

CONTENTS

THE FUTURE OF SEA POWER
IN THE PACIFIC

INTRODUCTION

THE Japanese denunciation of the Washington Treaty on December 29, 1934 announced the definitive collapse of the world's first serious attempt to meet the seemingly insoluble issues of modern navalism.[1] The history of this phenomenon is brief. Modern navalism—which is simply the eruption into the time-worn fields of maritime warfare of the intricate social, economic, political and technical forces released by the industrial age—can be assigned a beginning hardly earlier than the middle of the last century. Not until then was steam propulsion being generally introduced into the world's naval vessels. Save in their machinery spaces, the ships with which Perry appeared in Uraga Bay in 1853 differed in no essential from those in which the Portuguese had arrived in Japan three centuries before; while Perry's engines—a supplement to rather than a substitute for his lofty spars—had not yet chained him to the elaborate apparatus of fuel depots and repair bases by which the modern navy lives and moves. Not until about 1860 were the first experiments made with iron side-armor, turret mountings and mechanically trained artillery. Wood construction was not finally replaced by iron and steel until some years later; and only after 1880 did sail power dwindle at last into a vestigial remnant, and the mechanical navy of today emerge from its awkward age as the essentially new and dangerous instrument with which the world is now confronted.

The effects of this technical transformation were immediate, even though they were not immediately perceived. No longer was it possible to build powerful war vessels on almost any wooded estuary, man them with local fishermen or merchant sailors and dispatch them wherever wind and water served. To build and maintain the new navies required a relatively huge investment in iron mines,

1. For a brief summary of the Washington Treaty of 1922 and the London Treaty of 1930, cf. Appendix, p. 50.

steel works, gun and armor factories, dry docks and heavy machinery of all kinds. To keep them at sea demanded scattered systems of coaling stations and fortified bases. The personnel, not only of the ships but of the industries behind them, tended toward a greater specialization. Mobilization and demobilization became a slower and more difficult business; as a result, the new war machines tended for strategic reasons to be always upon a war footing, while a thickening crust of vested interest in their maintenance and expansion began to develop around them.

Naval officers found their whole careers dependent upon the enlargement of their service; the naval industries, once evoked to build a fleet, had to have continuing markets if their great investments were not to be lost and their workmen left unemployed. At the same time the new institution found itself equipped both with the unparalleled developmental resources of technology and with the commercial techniques of a world economy. Once scientific invention had been applied to naval warfare the progress was as swift, and as disrupting, as it had been elsewhere. The *U.S.S. Constitution*, completed in 1797, was just becoming obsolescent on the eve of the Civil War in 1860. The battleship *Indiana*, completed in 1895, was obsolescent on the eve of the World War, less than twenty years later. The British dreadnaught *Hercules*, completed in 1911, was "listed for disposal" prior to the Washington Conference in 1921, or after a life of only ten years. A constant succession of improvements authorized constantly recurrent demands upon the domestic taxpayer; intervals between home orders were filled by exploitation of the foreign market, and the fleets thus created abroad again stimulated sales at home. The new navalism thus spread through the world as rapidly as other aspects of the new industrialism, in much the same way and fundamentally, perhaps, for much the same reasons. Its principal cradle was Great Britain, and the British ship- and armament-builders thought themselves no more unnatural or unpatriotic in setting up competitive navalisms abroad than did the manufacturers of British cotton-mill machinery, for example, in establishing competitive cotton industries outside Britain.

I

THE MAHAN THEORY OF SEA POWER

BY about 1890 this new navalism had taken root in a dozen maritime countries; in most of them there were new heavy industries interested in or dependent upon naval orders, navalist politicians exploiting the glamors of this always enticing subject and groups of naval officers appealing to the civil power—with complete sincerity, it must be said—for the increasing appropriations necessary to sustain the intricate fleets now being elaborated. All were embarked, for their varying reasons, upon a process of rapid naval expansion; and there was urgent need for a rational justification of the process. The need, as so often happens, produced its own fulfillment. It was in the nineties that Captain Alfred Thayer Mahan, a scholarly officer of the American Navy (at the moment just beginning to arise from the all but complete extinction it had suffered after the Civil War), evolved the "sea power" theory of history. Swiftly expanded and enriched by naval men and naval propagandists all over the world, this theory provided the intellectual soil in which the new navalism was to flourish almost unchallenged down to the World War.

It was a rationalization ideally adjusted to the requirements of the case. It did not rest with its emphasis upon the importance of navies in the winning of wars, nor even with its assumption that the winning of wars was the decisive factor in the fate of peoples. It was more elaborate than that. It stressed, not actual naval battles, but that "command of the sea" assured to the possessor of the potential strength to win battles. It developed the significance of this "command of the sea" as a shield for maritime commerce in wartime, and thus provided an easy transition over which to carry these ideas into times of peace. By its mere existence in peace time a navy could still exercise "command of the sea," for it protected the national trade against the threat of war. This peaceable command of the sea, moreover, assured to a nation its foreign supplies and raw materials; it likewise assured it lucrative markets abroad. The theory thus simultaneously gave a new value to foreign commerce as a means to victory in war, and a new value to the apparatus of naval warfare as a means of promoting foreign commerce in peace time.

The new navies were bound much more closely to their bases than those of the past, and Mahan laid a special emphasis on the importance of outlying bases in the exercise of "command of the sea." But territories acquired for this reason might themselves be important sources of raw materials or valuable foreign markets. In this way the strategic needs of the navy and the economic needs of a developing domestic industry could be made nicely to interlock. Similarly, the navy required a merchant marine to support it in war; the merchant marine equally required a navy to defend it in peace, while the existence and expansion of both encouraged domestic industrial development, added to the national wealth and relieved the "pressure of population." "The due use and control of the sea," Mahan concluded, "is but one link in the chain of exchange by which wealth accumulates; but it is the central link, which lays under contribution other nations for the benefit of the one holding it, and which, history seems to assert, most surely of all gathers itself riches."

Captain Mahan did not, of course, originate many of the ideas which were woven into the doctrine; rather he merely synthesized the current needs and concepts of the politico-economic society about him into a general rationale of navalism. Nor can he be blamed for the many shaky edifices of deductive reasoning raised by his disciples upon the foundation thus provided. The result, however, was a complete system, adequate to justify the peace-time competition in building, the geometrically expanding appropriations, the scramble for overseas bases, the international truculences and trade rivalries, which the new institution by its very nature demanded. Navalism had been given its place in the setting of late nineteenth century industrial expansion; the slogan had been proclaimed that "the navy pays!" The assumptions upon which the theory rested were often concealed, and frequently in violent conflict with other assumptions which continued to rule at the same time in the press, parliaments and national policies of the world. Within its assumptions, however, the theory was sound enough. Undoubtedly the new navies did "pay" large and influential classes —owners and employees of heavy industry, colonial proconsuls and officeholders, nationalist politicians as well as naval men—very directly; while even in the larger accounting of national welfare and general public interest they paid, too, upon occasion, though perhaps in currency of a doubtful permanence. From the publication of *The Influence of Sea Power on History* in 1890 until the moment, on June 21, 1919, when the waters of Scapa Flow closed ingloriously over one of its mightiest creations, modern navalism swept onward through its golden age.

II

PRE-WAR NAVALISM IN THE PACIFIC

PERHAPS the two powers which were seemingly to profit most and suffer least from navalism were the United States and Japan. In spite of the relatively greater maturity of American industry, the new navalism took root in both countries at about the same time and followed in some respects a closely parallel development. Japan was forced into the Western economic system by the use of naval power; and it was a direct instinct of self-preservation in a strange world which led her to ask that world for naval armaments first of all. The Western powers were only too glad to avail themselves of the profitable opportunity to supply her; and by 1860 Great Britain, Holland, France and the United States were cooperating with gifts of ships, technical advice and experts to found the Japanese Navy. In 1864, ironically enough, the same four powers also cooperated in the bombardment of Shimonoseki—an episode which in no way interrupted their efforts to furnish Japan with the weapons that were very soon to render such chastisements inadvisable.

The first important Western industry in Japan was a naval ship-yard, and though the Japanese continued to purchase foreign-built war vessels down to the World War, they earnestly devoted themselves from the first to the creation of a domestic naval armaments industry. Indeed, it was primarily in order to equip the country with modern armaments that Japanese heavy industry was originally established, and it is still far more dependent upon armament orders than are the heavy industries of older economies. In the United States, on the other hand, there was an opposite development. Our industrialization arose upon such activities as railroad building and factory equipment; our naval shipyards, armor plate and gun plants came late in our economic history, and are still a much less significant element in the American scene. Occupied with the exploitation of the West, it was long before we began to think seriously of foreign industrial markets or the glamors of imperialism. We did not take up the new navalism in earnest until the middle eighties; we were then without equipment for the manufacture of armor, and we had to secure plans for some of our first vessels from Great Britain. Japan was by that time industriously buying similar ships from the British and French and developing her own facilities for building and manning them.

Because of our much greater resources and technical experience, we were naturally able to free ourselves from dependence on foreign sources much more quickly than the Japanese. The two fleets, however, grew more or less together. In 1890 and 1892 we authorized the construction of four battleships—the first in the American Navy. In 1893 Japan adopted a five-year naval program calling for the purchase of four battleships, as well as corresponding vessels of the lesser classes. Two of the smaller cruisers, incidentally, were bought in the United States. In 1894-95 Japan's new weapons received their first test in the Sino-Japanese War; it was a brilliantly successful affair, no less from the political than from the military point of view. Japan emerged with greatly enhanced prestige, a dominant position over all other Asiatic powers, a fresh confidence in the virtues of navalism, but with a sense of having been robbed of her victory by a West whom she was not yet strong enough to challenge. The navy was in a new position of influence in the state. The 1893 program was promptly expanded.

The United States underwent a similar experience in 1898. We, likewise, emerged from our victory over Spain with an enhanced prestige, an unassailable position in the Western Hemisphere, a new confidence in "sea power" (it had alone made our easy victory possible), a new enthusiasm for imperialist adventure and an awakened suspicion of the European powers who seemed still to regard the Caribbean as within their spheres of policy. Our navy, like the Japanese, spoke with greater authority in public affairs. Where Japanese naval men could point to the Russian danger, our own could cite (though perhaps less impressively) the need for protecting the new base in the Philippine Islands; and we also enlarged our naval building.

In both these wars the victor's navy had "paid." It was to do so even more spectacularly in the Russo-Japanese War of 1904-05. Again the "sea power" theory received what seemed a brilliant confirmation. "Command of the sea" alone enabled the Japanese to isolate and defeat the Russian forces in the Far East. The victory not only removed a threat to Japanese independence; it also brought new markets, new raw material supplies, new land wherewith to "relieve the pressure of population." The war itself greatly stimulated the processes of industrialization, brought new wealth to many, deepened the incrustation of vested interest upon the institutions of navalism and imperialism. Later on it was also to bring depression and taxation in its train; while it left Japan suddenly exposed upon a world stage before powers which, once friendly and encouraging, quickly began to assume attitudes of suspicion and hostility. Some possible defects of the sea power theory were casting their shadows before. But under the theory itself—and this was one of its greatest elements of strength—the cure for navalism was more navalism. Depression at home could only make more urgent the demand for fresh naval construction, just as hostility abroad called for more ships, a greater "command of the sea," and better protection for trade and markets. The Japanese naval shipbuilding industry was now fully established. Save for the battle cruiser *Kongo,* bought in England as a pattern ship of a new type, no men-of-war were ordered from abroad after the Russo-Japanese War. Once more Japanese navalism enlarged its scope. "Japan was obliged," according to Captain Hironori Mizuno, "to expand her naval policy, hitherto confined to the Yellow and the Japan Seas, so as to comprehend the Pacific Ocean in its strategy." Unavoidably, it helped to stimulate the expansion of navalism in the United States, whose strategy also "comprehended" the Pacific Ocean.

For the first time, the Japanese and American navalisms were brought, so to speak, into direct contact. Like the principal European powers, the United States had for many years maintained a small "Asiatic Squadron" in Far Eastern waters; we also retained a few ships and shore stations along the Pacific Coast—doubtless more in deference to the importunities of local interests than for any strategic end they might have served. As early as 1897 the possibility of an American-Japanese war had occurred at least to Theodore Roosevelt; and one of the arguments for our retention of the Philippines after the Spanish-American War in 1898 was the desirability of forestalling the Japanese. It was only after Japan's dramatic triumph over Russia, however, that the two navalisms seriously began to adopt each other as possible rivals, and that the patterns of competitive hostility, inevitable in such situations, began definitely to take form.

NAVAL COMPETITION ON A WORLD SCALE

For navalism was entering a new phase. Up to this time Great Britain alone had attempted to maintain anything approaching the general "command of the sea" which the Mahan doctrine held to be vital to national success. Beneath the shadow of British supremacy the other navies had existed as primarily local forces, all more or less equal and none competent to "command" more than a very limited area of sea in its own neighborhood. The larger objectives of the theory, being impossible of attainment, had been easily dispensed with. Now, however, these objectives were imposing themselves upon the course of events. Competition was being transferred from a local to a world stage. While the smaller and poorer navies resigned themselves to a negligible importance, the three or four greatest fleets were coming into direct opposition to each other. The Germans made their challenge to Great Britain. The United States, while confronted by the great European armadas beyond its eastern seaboard, suddenly realized that in its western ocean, also, there was a fleet not greatly inferior to its own, in the hands of a power quite as energetic and aggressive as itself.

For no very good reason other than the emotional reactions which these great displays of armed force set up, there was a real Japanese "war scare" in 1907. At that time the Panama Canal was not yet open, and it was only after the World War that we were to transfer our battle fleet permanently to the Pacific and make that ocean the center of our naval activity. In 1908, however, the fleet was dispatched upon its cruise around the world, with the object, apparently, of overawing the new Japanese naval power. The Japanese were studiously polite; but the result was of course the opposite of that intended, and both navalisms made renewed demands upon their taxpayers.

It was at this point, however, that the first great technical revolution supervened. The dreadnaught battleship, a type enormously superior to the vessels which had preceded it, now appeared, to be quickly seized upon by the naval constructors of all the maritime powers. The great fleets of pre-dreadnaughts which had by this time accumulated were to be rendered obsolete within a space of two or three years, and in the race for "command of the sea" all the nations were in effect returned to scratch. At the same time the race had been rendered considerably more expensive, and the American public began to lose interest in its always rather synthetic attractions. Navalism, conveniently enough, is never required to state the precise objectives which it is to serve, or present any exact calculation of costs and benefits in support of its demands. The values in which the navy is supposed to pay are of a vague and general character, insusceptible to any definite measurement. The investment necessary to produce them is equally beyond scientific determination. All warfare is a gamble; it is impossible to say with confidence that a given amount of naval equipment will certainly achieve any given purpose, and as a result modern naval expansion has always been untrammeled by any narrow limitations of policy. But it also follows that naval programs are very vulnerable to a change in the public mood; and after Theodore Roosevelt's departure from the Presidency in 1909 the American naval effort perceptibly slackened. That of Japan was, if anything, intensified.

At the beginning of the dreadnaught era, about 1909, the United States had amassed a fleet of twenty-five pre-dreadnaught battleships, while the Japanese possessed only eleven. But by 1913 the United States had built or building only thirteen of the new dreadnaught type, while the Japanese had nine built or under way. It should be pointed out, however, that naval statistics, despite their appearance of unanswerable solidity, are actually very fluid quantities, lending themselves admirably to the uses of special pleading. It is for this reason that they so often differ between one compilation and another. The comparison here given, for example, involves certain transitional ships, neither dreadnaughts nor pre-dreadnaughts, and the figures might be altered by allocating these differently between the classes. I have tried to adopt the fairest presentation, but am aware that almost any use of naval statistics is open to argument.

In the spring of 1913 there was another transient war scare over the California land laws, there was an intensification of naval building in Europe, and presently there came the intervention at Vera Cruz. In the first half of 1914 Congress appropriated for double the amount of tonnage voted in the preceding year, including three dreadnaughts in place of one. American navalism was reviving. But where this new movement might have led it is possible only to conjecture, for in August 1914 the European War—prepared at least in part by the Anglo-German naval rivalry of the previous half-dozen years—burst upon the world.

III

THE FIRST CRISIS OF MODERN NAVALISM

JAPAN'S CHALLENGE TO THE UNITED STATES AND GREAT BRITAIN

ITS effect on naval history was to be a curious one. When in August 1914 Admiral Mahan urged Great Britain into the holocaust in strict accordance with the doctrine which was his life work, he can scarcely have anticipated that the result of British victory would be the passage of maritime supremacy from British hands. He can hardly have calculated that the chief beneficiaries of the triumph (from the narrow viewpoint of "sea power") would be Japan and the United States. Yet such was the outcome. The land war engrossed all the energies of Russia, Austria, Italy and France, and they simply abandoned the contest for "command of the sea." The British and German navalisms were locked in their great struggle to destroy one another. In the United States, on the other hand, the dangers, the problems and the fascinations of the European War generated an extraordinary wave of militarist sentiment, which the British themselves frequently did their best to encourage as a possible aid against the Germans. The material and emotional forces favorable to naval expansion, always latent in the modern industrial state, were suddenly provided with an immense leverage over public opinion; and in the summer of 1916 the American Congress authorized an enormous program of naval shipbuilding. It was to be compressed into three years only, and the tonnage to be laid down in the first year alone was some four times the average of preceding years.

The precise ends which this great program was designed to serve remain buried in the fogs of naval metaphysics that surrounded its inception. The clearest ostensible reason for it was to defend the United States (or at any rate the integrity of the Monroe Doctrine) against an attack by Germany in case the latter should emerge victorious from the war. There was, however, little if any intelligent discussion of the likelihood, or even the possibility, of such an attack. There was no remotely scientific calculation of the naval strength which might be necessary to repel one. On the part of public opinion there seems to have been little more than a general feeling that it would be desirable to have a greater naval power; on the part of the naval experts there seems to have been little more than a conviction that it would be desirable to have as great an increase as possible. The program bore no practical relation to the European War itself, for when we entered the conflict eight months later the whole thing was tossed aside. The heavy ships for which it called were useless against a German battle fleet already immobilized, and it was necessary to bend every energy to the construction of destroyers and merchantmen to meet the submarine danger. When the war ended in the destruction of the German Navy the principal reason for the 1916 program had disappeared. But the program itself had not. A few of the ships had been laid down; authorizations and appropriations for the others were available. Work upon them was immediately resumed.

Simultaneously with the United States, Japan also had adopted a 1916 program, practically identical in size, although its construction was to be spread over a longer period of time. Both programs called for a battle line of eight superdreadnaughts and eight battle cruisers, with auxiliary types in addition. Under the original plan, ours would have been complete by the end of 1922; Japan's by the end of 1927. Again the British, in utilizing Japan's assistance against Germany, had encouraged the new essay in navalism. It may be doubted whether anyone in Japan had a much more precise idea of what it was to accomplish than had anyone in the United States with respect to our own effort; but just as the United States expected her program to maintain her supremacy in the Western Hemisphere, so Japan probably intended hers to make her supreme in the Western Pacific. In 1914 and 1915 she had seized the opportunity afforded by the war to initiate an aggressively imperialist policy on the Asiatic mainland. Her navalists could argue, with considerable logic, that a formidable navy would be required to preserve this policy from the Western interference it was pretty sure to arouse. Actually, the interference came long before the ships could be ready, and the policy was, for the time being, largely abandoned. But in Japan, as in the United States, a flood tide of war prosperity had made the adoption of a costly building program easy; when the war ended and the tide receded, naval work supplied a useful "cushion" of orders and employment, and in the end a naval program originally advanced as an instrument of policy survived to become a policy in itself. Japan was dedicated to the pursuit of "sea power" on a scale now rivaled by only two other nations in the world.

In June 1919 the German crews at Scapa Flow opened the seacocks of their floating fortresses and the great High Seas Fleet—on which so vast an energy had been expended, because of which millions of lives had been sacrificed—vanished from the seas, never once having been brought into a decisive action. The "battle of the shipyards," that curious product of the Mahanite teaching, had ended; the British had achieved at last the total destruction of the rival "sea power." But as they looked up exhausted from their victory, it was to perceive that in winning it they had helped call into existence not one but two new "sea powers," each quite as formidable as that which had gone. The British, staggering under a colossal debt, were seeking only to demobilize their war effort, and they had no new building under way. Both the American and the Japanese shipyards were humming with activity. Great Britain could count an effective battle line of but thirty-one heavy ships; the United States had thirty-five either built, on the ways or about to be begun; Japan had nineteen built or building and eight more projected, to give a total of twenty-seven.

Nor was that all. There had been a second technical revolution. Aviation was adding a whole new, and very costly, element to the time-honored apparatus of maritime war. The Grand Fleet which had fought at Jutland was already obsolescent before the new American and Japanese monsters. The "post-Jutland" dreadnaught was as superior to the earlier vessels of the class as the first dreadnaughts had been to the battleships of Santiago and Tsu-Shima. When the new programs were complete, the United States and Japan would each possess sixteen of these powerful weapons, Great Britain only one. Apparently it was all to be done over again; and the British, obedient to the strict dictates of "sea power," turned to the preparation of still more colossal battleships, which would outclass the American and Japanese tonnage as the latter threatened to outclass the war navy of Great Britain.

MAHAN THEORY QUESTIONED

But in the great aftermath of the World War it was impossible not to feel serious doubts as to the adequacy of the sea power theory of history. Were there not vital factors in the problem which that theory had failed to take into consideration? On purely technical grounds, even, it was open to question. The World War had, if anything, overemphasized the economic and maritime elements in warfare; but at the same time it had undermined the more abstract and mystical conceptions of "sea power" as a quality resting magically, like the locks of Samson, on the shoulders of the nation which could claim the longest battle line or the most impressive pictures in the pages of *Jane's Fighting Ships*. With the appearance of the submarine and aviation were "command of the sea" and "defense of trade" any longer possible, no matter how great the battle line supremacy a nation might amass? The mighty apparatus of sea power on which Germany had strained her resources was nearly useless to her in the war and ultimately proved her Achilles' heel; her submarines, on the other hand, came very near to establishing an actual command of the sea of a sort upon which Mahan had never calculated. The merely technical problem was apparently far more complex than anything envisioned by the propagandas of peacetime naval competition.

This discovery might have served only to prompt the major navalisms to still greater efforts had the theory in its other aspects remained unimpaired. But the costs which it must ultimately impose were now seen to be staggering in size. By emphasizing the peace-time importance of "sea power" it had in effect made warfare continuous, waged with competitive building in the intervals when it was not being waged upon the battlefield. In this rivalry no power could halt without surrender; while the rapidity of technical advance—tending toward a situation in which one fleet would no sooner be completed than another would have to be begun to meet improvements introduced elsewhere in the meantime—seemed to promise that no power could ever win. Nor did there appear to be any logical end to the process. It began at last to dawn upon world opinion that the general philosophy of imperialism, and the sea power theory which was its special derivative, contained no limiting factors within themselves. Since the sea power theory was simply a rationalization of world conflict, it naturally could lead to no other conclusion. By their very nature, its assumptions provided no check upon peace-time naval expansion until it had absorbed the entire energies of the state; they admitted of no finality save bankruptcy or war. In 1919 and 1920 war was seen to be a far more frightful and disastrous business than it had appeared to be in the golden age of navalism ten years before; and there was felt to be an inherent absurdity in a concept of national interest and historical causation which doomed great peoples inevitably to such a fate.

If the pains of navalism had become more severe, its promised benefits were now seen, though less clearly, to be dubious. Even before the war the assumptions of economic imperialism were already under attack, not only from the Marxist but from the classic Liberal viewpoint; and in 1910 Norman Angell had struck the first important blow at their specifically military application, though the real bearing of his argument was largely overlooked. Now embarrassing questions began to form with an urgency not to be denied. Was it really necessary to conquer raw material supplies when they might be had by the much easier method of buying them? Was it rational to prepare to fight for markets when all the most valuable markets were actually provided by the other great industrial states with whom the wars would have to be fought? After Great Britain had destroyed, by a fearful effort, her principal trade rival, her first discovery was that she had likewise destroyed one of her most lucrative customers, and much of her policy in the immediate post-war years was devoted to reviving the industrialism she had just overthrown. Was it necessary to protect a foreign trade transacted so largely with the nations alone equipped to attack it?

In a speech before the Japanese Diet on January 22, 1935, Mr. Hirota, the Foreign Minister, observed that Japan and the United States are bound "by a vital economic relationship of mutual inter-dependence unparalleled elsewhere." Certainly, the inconsistency of our fighting a war with Japan to protect our Far Eastern markets appears in the fact that Japan herself provided 51 per cent of those markets in 1933. Our total trade (imports and exports) with Japan amounted to 39 per cent of our total Far Eastern trade and 9 per cent of our world trade. Among all countries, Japan is our third best customer. An added irony of the situation is found in the fact that a lucrative, if relatively minor, part of these exports is devoted to arming Japan. The absurdities which can arise in these matters are well illustrated by the case of the Japanese naval officer recently taken into custody in Florida. The public was shocked to hear that he had actually been photographing Florida harbors—of no possible military importance—but saw nothing alarming in the fact that he was stationed in this country as an inspector of military supplies which we are regularly shipping to our theoretical enemy!

But even more searching questions than the protection of foreign trade could be asked. What, actually, was "population pressure," and how far was it ever in fact "relieved" through military action? Was there not, indeed, some profound inconsistency in the whole mer-cantilist concept of "foreign markets," under which industrialist states desperately competed in dumping into the hands of foreigners "surpluses" which might better have gone to raising domestic stand-ards of living?

By 1920 modern navalism, standing amid the universal ruin which it had in part produced, had reached its first crisis. It was committing the major naval powers to a renewal of the whole effort on a greater and apparently an ever-expanding scale. Their finances were shaky; their peoples war-weary and reluctant. The sole visible end of the process was a grim one; the prizes it offered were beginning to seem hollow; the basic assumptions on which it rested were coming into question. The materials, at least, were present for constructing a wholly new theory of naval armaments, a new and fundamentally different rationalization of the essential relations between modern industrial states. Unhappily, the collective thought and statesmanship of the world were unequal to so arduous a task. The conference at Washington in 1921, like the Paris Peace Conference, did not attempt to uproot the matted growths of tradition, established ideas and vested interests which were forcing the world to a new outburst of navalism. Instead, it sought only to imprison them within the fragile limits of the *status quo*.

IV

NAVALISM IN A STRAITJACKET

THE WASHINGTON COMPROMISE

THE compromises embodied in the Washington treaties admittedly rested upon no principle more profound than that of calling a halt. The celebrated 5-5-3 ratio was calculated upon no absolute considerations of naval strategy, defense requirements or national policy. It was derived from the simple fact that the various building programs had actually worked out, through the interplay of the many chance factors determining their adoption and prosecution, to give at that moment completed battle-line strengths about in that proportion. It had no higher claim to validity, but it possessed—at a time when no power could face a new naval race with any confidence—the great merit of simple pragmatism. It required no great sacrifice by any of the powers of the relative strength which they actually had in hand at the time; it accorded roughly with what the various publics had been taught to regard as their appropriate naval requirements, and it proved a practicable basis for a truce.

This naval truce demanded a formal surrender by Great Britain of her traditional "two-power standard" and a formal surrender by the United States of the right to contest for predominance. It was also accompanied by a series of political settlements in which the stability of the Far East was in effect entrusted to a self-denying ordinance on the part of Japan. Whether these political settlements were, as is so often said, the indispensable condition which made possible the naval truce, or whether it was in reality the naval truce which made possible the political settlements, may be open to question, but at all events it is probably irrelevant. A halt was called all around. The five navies affected were laced into the straitjackets of what happened to be the *status quo,* there to remain—in so far as anything in the treaty system provided—forever. The treaty structure thus represented a very considerable limitation upon what might be called the pure theory of imperialism and sea power. Yet the many and complex forces which had produced these great navalisms, and which must necessarily work toward their continuous expansion, were left almost untouched. In none of the five powers did the basic doctrines of the sea power theory meet any effective challenge; in all they continued to be taught by naval propagandas and very largely to rule whenever the naval estimates happened to come up for parliamentary approval. In the wisdom of after knowledge it is not very difficult to see, perhaps, that the collapse of the truce was inevitable.

The collapse began very quickly—the first fissures, indeed, appearing at the conference itself. The Japanese delegation sought to improve a little upon the existing position and so get one hitch ahead of the others. It appealed to the convenient metaphysics of strategy. Its studies in that imprecise realm, it said, forced it to the conclusion that Japan required a ratio not of 3 but of 3.5. The adroit compromise concerning the further fortification of Eastern naval bases surmounted this difficulty. More serious was the resistance of the French. France was unprepared for the financial sacrifice which would have been demanded by any attempt to rival the mighty battle lines of Great Britain, the United States and Japan. She was willing enough to abide by her weak position in regard to heavy ships. Her naval men, however, with a realistic appreciation of the true lessons of the war, understood the great potentialities of the lighter weapons—submarines, destroyers, light cruisers and aviation —as instruments for exerting a very effective sea power regardless of the battle lines which under the Mahan theory were supposed to be supreme. France refused to accept a permanent inferiority in these types.

The French thus rejected the basic principle—perpetuation of the *status quo*—upon which the whole truce rested. And in thus undermining the ideology of the structure they also opened the way whereby it was to be destroyed in practice. Down to the World War naval competition had concerned itself almost entirely with battle-line strength. Naval propagandas centered public attention upon the heavy ships of rival powers—the vessels which were to fight the fleet actions or make up the invincible "fleets in being" whereby "command of the sea" was to be decided. All the lighter types were lumped together as "auxiliaries," and as the name suggests were usually thought of as auxiliary elements within the battle fleet organization —lesser cogs in the main fighting machine—rather than as independent instruments of commerce destruction or defense, with independent missions of their own. The number of "auxiliaries" would consequently depend in the first instance upon the number of battle-line units which they served. The German submarine war was a brilliant refutation of this concept of maritime conflict; nevertheless, Secretary Hughes still clung to it in making his famous opening proposal at the Washington Conference. Having determined the 5-5-3 ratio on the basis of existing battle-line strength, he then assumed that this ratio would be an appropriate measure of auxiliary tonnage as well, although the existing position in regard to auxiliaries departed very widely from the battleship ratios. It was the French insistence, in effect, upon a free hand in the lighter categories which rendered this rough-and-ready—and somewhat inconsistent—attempt at limiting cruisers, destroyers and submarines abortive. In the end the lighter categories escaped all limitation; and very soon the competition which had been halted in the matter of battleships was duly transferred to this department. Here the rival navalisms continued to expand as before, the more freely because they no longer had to meet the heavy financial burden of battleship building.

Naval writers were everywhere quick to discover that "auxiliary" tonnage was not really auxiliary at all, but of vital importance in the independent operations of patrolling lines of communication or threatening enemy commerce. Oddly enough, American navalists perceived that the 5-5-3 ratio, originally deduced as a pragmatic measure of battle fleet "needs," was likewise an exact measure of our needs in these other branches of naval warfare. With this discovery both British and Japanese naval men, however, were slow to agree. The Japanese could see little merit in a method of reasoning which would have confined them to a permanent inferiority in types not controlled by the Washington Treaty; while the British developed a theory of absolute rather than relative requirements where cruisers were concerned—a theory which, by a strange coincidence, worked out to confirm them in the overwhelming superiority in cruisers which they happened to possess.

Despite the contrary implications of the Washington structure, the basic sea power theory was thus preserved in almost its full force and effect. It remained as an accepted system of ideas quite adequate to support a vigorous naval competition even within the life of the treaties, and an unlimited expansion of navalism thereafter up to the point of whatever smash might result. Again, as before, it was not required to justify itself by any exact definition of national policy. There are few national policies from which the need for a greater navy may not be deduced; and it is seldom that a greater navy does not in itself lead to an extension of national policy. It was after the Washington Conference that the Navy Department adopted as an appropriate object of American naval strength the exercise of "ocean-wide economic pressure"—something which our naval propagandas of the pre-war years would scarcely have dared even to suggest. Again, as before, expansion was promoted by special interests of one sort or another within the various powers—professional naval men and navalist politicians, jingoistic newspapers, ship- and armament-builders, labor leaders concerned with the shipping trades, exporters, business men abroad feeling the need of prestige to support their salesmanship. It is interesting that when the British Labor Government, by authorizing the new cruiser program of 1924, took the first important step toward the resumption of active competition, it was justified by the pacifist Prime Minister, Mr. Ramsay MacDonald, on the ground that it would afford employment for shipyard workers. The celebrated William B. Shearer probably took too great a credit upon himself when he claimed alone to have wrecked the 1927 naval conference, but there is no doubt that this paid agent of the American shipbuilders exerted all his influence against any agreement which would have restricted American naval building. And it is evident that in the latter stages of the treaty period the desire of the Japanese Navy not to be outdone by the Army in the contest for political power in the state intensified the pressure for naval expansion.

Such immediate, and wholly domestic, considerations of personal ambition or material gain are too subtly interwoven with larger emotional factors, with loose ideas of patriotism and national interest, with uncritical popular responses, to permit of any assessment of their true importance. It is enough to say that they are of much less real weight than the conventional pacifist supposes, but of much greater influence than his opponent will admit. At all events it took some time for the fears and exhaustions of 1921 to pass and for the forces favorable to navalism to reassert themselves in a renewed naval race. The intellectual, emotional and material apparatus was ready, however, and after 1925 it was seen to be grinding again in earnest. In 1927 the "Coolidge" Conference at Geneva made its futile attempt to halt the process; in 1930, at the cost of considerable effort and by a series of ingenious compromises, the London Conference just succeeded in extending the Washington ratio system to the light tonnage of Great Britain, the United States and Japan. The cruisers, destroyers and submarines of these three powers were barely squeezed at last into the framework of limitation—though in a way which notably left all three at liberty to indulge in a very large measure of further building.

The very text of the London Treaty, however, announced more plainly than was recognized at the time the ultimate end of the ratio system. The Japanese by a vigorous struggle got their ratio for the "auxiliary" categories enlarged from the 3 of Washington to about 3.5, and then explicitly stated that their acceptance of the new figures was without prejudice to future demands. This could only mean that unless Japan should thereafter alter her policy the treaty system must fail; and the difficulty of inducing any modern power to alter a foreign policy except under duress or by "compensation" is familiar to everyone. More than that, where the Washington Treaty had imposed an agreed status over a period of ten years, the London Treaty ran for only five; while so far from establishing the new ratios at the beginning of this shorter time, it merely provided a schedule under which they would be arrived at just as the treaty expired. The navies need not actually be reduced to the agreed limits until the day before they would be freed, by the expiration of the treaty, from limitation of any sort. It was a device which made it absolutely essential that the treaty system be extended before that date arrived, but the mechanism for doing so was seriously defective. Finally, it proved impossible to bring either France or Italy within the new framework; while the naval adjustment was accompanied by none of those political settlements which had been effected at Washington. In effect, the Washington truce was barely prolonged through the expedient of postponing for later settlement nearly all the issues which it was raising.

These issues were grave; the onset of world depression was to make them graver still and to intensify the pressures with which the navalist system was already striving to burst the paper bonds imposed upon it. At Washington the United States and Great Britain had renounced the pure practice of maritime imperialism (as between each other) just far enough to admit of a co-equal "supremacy," and at London this renunciation was confirmed. In every other respect they, like the remaining powers involved, had accepted and acted upon the basic assumptions of the sea power theory. Their delegations did not question the importance of "command of the sea," the necessity or possibility of "defending" trade, markets and interests abroad, the value of prestige, the reality of that kind of paper "dominance" determined by the computation of tonnage tables rather than the actual possibilities of war. Around the conference table the United States and Great Britain, no less than Japan, played the conventional rôle of aggressively imperialist states, seeking to maintain their own naval greatness and to suppress any challenge from others. Such is the face which all powers customarily assume before the world when engaged in international negotiations; in the privacy of their domestic political and economic organizations, however, there may be differences between them, and for a variety of reasons navalism may be said to have taken a much stronger effective hold over Japanese national policy than over the policies of the United States and Great Britain.

BREAKDOWN OF THE RATIO SYSTEM

In Japan the navalist assumptions were more implicitly believed in, more readily translated into practice, less confused by contrary economic or historical rationalizations. Japan is a power still relatively weak both in resources and prestige, and for that reason is not greatly impressed by the pacific impulses of nations already standing upon the pinnacles of military strength and industrial greatness. From the beginning of her career in the Western world, everything she has achieved has seemed to come through military victory and conquest. Her economic organization, as compared with that of the United States or Great Britain, is in a primitive or at any rate a youthful stage. For this reason a rapid increase of industrial volume, regardless of the immediate credit balance, may be of greater real importance to her; and a policy of forcible annexation of foreign markets may have a genuine, if short-run, economic validity in her case which it would lack in the case of the other two. Her want of raw materials makes her far more vulnerable to an interruption of her sea-borne commerce than the United States and perhaps no less so than Great Britain. Her military industries are, as has been said, a much more significant element of her industrial structure. It is true that Japan is still a predominantly agrarian state, but the only challenge to the control of policy by the industrialists has come from the military men. Her military organizations now hold a much more commanding position in domestic politics than is the case with the United States or Great Britain, and a larger and more influential part of the population finds its future dependent upon the steady expansion of the army and navy. Finally, Japan (like the United States) has never had to sustain the terrible and paralyzing exhaustion of a modern major war. On all counts, the immediate gains promised by navalism are more real for Japan than for other powers; its possible penalties are more remote.

Since the check received in 1921 and 1922, Japan has followed the navalist-imperialist tradition with a single-mindedness and consistency not observable in the policies of the older powers. The Washington settlements soon entered into domestic politics, and the nationalist and militarist elements used them as a means of overthrowing the more moderate capitalist politicians responsible for their ratification. The earthquake of 1923 aggravated the economic strains of the post-war period; and these were met by naval and armament orders, subsidies and credit inflation at home, and by forcing exports at a terrific pace. Where the United States was content to give away her "surpluses" through the medium of uncollectible foreign loans, Japan resorted to the more direct method of drastic price competition, intensified with the onset of the depression by an extreme debasement of her currency. She was also the first important industrial power to resort to the device of deficit-budgeting on a grand scale; but her whole economic policy has been the old mercantilist one of sustaining industrial activity by governmental favors to the owning classes on the one hand, and by capturing foreign markets on the other, regardless of any broad national profit-and-loss accounting or of the actual returns they may yield toward an immediate increase in the domestic standard of living. With the Mukden incident in 1931 this policy began to translate itself, precisely as had happened with the older imperialisms, into aggressive military action of the "colonial war" type—where "expansion," the conquest of new territory, new markets and raw material supplies could be achieved at a negligible cost in life and through an industrial effort which itself tended, in the short run, to stimulate rather than to strain the domestic economy.

It would require an exhaustive study of the inner causes of the Japanese Army's assault upon Manchuria and the Japanese Navy's assault upon Shanghai to establish the true relationship between these phenomena and the economic position of Japan. Doubtless it is a more subtle and indirect one than is usually supposed—less a case of an economic cause producing a military effect than of an interaction between economic and military factors, each reinforcing the other in the direction of a common end. However that may be, the practical result has been to render a further continuation of the 1922 settlement out of the question. One must not overlook the fact that the settlement was being undermined from other directions as well. The revival of German navalism has already had serious repercussions in France and Italy; the precarious balance between the two latter powers now seems to have been upset, and a kind of three-cornered naval race to be working up in Continental waters. Such a development must sooner or later have affected the British and so transmitted its shocks and strains to the limitation structure erected by the three leading naval powers. Professional British naval opinion itself has for some time been showing an increasing restlessness under the restrictions of Washington and London, and though the government has refused to yield to this agitation it has not helped the treaty system. Where their purely naval policies were concerned, all the powers have clung to a concept of history and of international relations which must sooner or later have fractured the truce of 1922. But it seems not unfair to say that it is the Japanese, applying that concept with a much greater earnestness in practice, who have actually forced the pace.

Much of the material with which Japanese military and naval writers, "Foreign Office spokesmen" and the like have not only justified the Japanese case but have developed it to a point calling for an entire "nation in arms" with all its energies concentrated upon war, will strike the American or British reader as the most grotesque and shocking absurdity. Yet, like the similar material produced in Nazi Germany, it actually only carries to an extreme logical conclusion the general system of ideas which governs the military and naval policy and to a lesser extent the diplomacy of all the great armed powers. If this sort of teaching seems to be Mahan reduced to the absurd, it is because the absurdity was inherent in the original doctrine. A recent Japanese War Office pamphlet, to take a random example, supports its argument for vast additional military preparation with the observation that "the military strength of the Empire is a sane, powerful force, with which to crush evil actions and heretical doctrines, and thereby to declare the Empire's law of justice before the world. This military force radically differs from that of other nations who use their military forces for the realization of their selfish purposes and who are always eager to attain a superior position in all spheres of activity." It is easy to smile at such naïveté. But does it differ so much, at bottom, from Mr. Norman Davis's recent assertion of our claim to naval superiority over Japan on the ground that "the aim to which the United States is dedicated is to be a good neighbor, respecting the rights of all nations both weak and strong and to cooperate in the promotion of world peace and progress"? Or with the frank, and public, assumption of American naval men that our navy must be strong enough to fight Japan in her home waters? I think it would not be difficult to show that the most extreme manifestations of contemporary Japanese (and German) militarism can be logically justified by ideas and attitudes which pass almost without question in the more "pacific" powers.

In 1930 Japan reserved her rights under the London Treaty, and so gave notice that the naval settlement was on the way to extinction. In 1931 she destroyed the force of the political agreements which had accompanied it. In 1933 she announced her withdrawal from the League of Nations, and so dissociated herself from another aspect of the great post-war effort (of which the Washington Conference was only a part) to solve the basic problems of militarism and war by a simple perpetuation of the *status quo*. In 1934 she formally rejected the ratio system of naval limitation and exercised her right to denounce the Washington Treaty itself. In the Pacific, as elsewhere in the world society, the dynamic forces in human affairs had burst the straitjackets which statesmanship had sought to impose upon them. That apparent solution for the problem of modern navalism—seeming so admirable when it was devised and serving throughout a decade at least well enough to conceal its own superficiality—was in ruins; and the major naval powers found themselves back, in effect, at the point where they had stood in 1920. The London treaty may still maintain the truce until its expiration in December 1936; but beyond there is now nothing save the inherently uncontrollable processes of naval competition, exacting their geometrically increasing sacrifices of money and effort and holding out no ultimate conclusion save the probable catastrophe of a major war. Modern navalism has arrived at its second crisis.

V

THE ALTERNATIVES BEFORE US

WHAT this crisis really "means" to the various nations, in terms of practical well-being for the masses of individual men and women who compose them, it is impossible even to ask. The values in which the necessary equations would have to be constructed are immeasurable. One can, for example, assign a money value to those American "interests" in the Far East which

American navalism is supposed to protect; but one cannot calculate even the money costs of an attempt to protect them in this way, one can hazard only the vaguest of guesses as to whether the attempt would in the long run actually result in their protection, while the money value of the interests is useless as a measure of their real worth to the great body of American citizens. No doubt Japan, to take a different example, can progressively free herself from military or diplomatic interference by a *relative* increase of her naval power; but it is quite impossible (notwithstanding the confident prophecies of her Minister of the Navy) for her to estimate with any accuracy the chances of emerging from a naval race with a relative gain. Even less can she calculate the long-run benefits to be derived by her population as a whole from a freedom thus acquired. Perhaps some of the anticipated benefits would prove to be real; others, however, might well turn out to be fictitious and still others might more easily and surely be attained in a different way—through simple trade penetration, for instance. There is no possible method for striking sound balances in these vague and emotion-ridden realms.

For this reason no attempt is here made to deal with the present crisis as a conflict of simple and sharply-defined national interests, susceptible to evaluation and therefore to compromise. Indeed, the very nature of the crisis itself precludes such treatment. The difficulty lies not in any specific international *impasse,* but in the character of the institution of navalism as a whole. It arises from no sudden aberration in the workings of the navalist process, but from the fact that the ends to which this process is now seen naturally to lead have become unattractive, even unbearable, to large numbers of people. If the assumptions in which it advances were unchallenged, there would be no crisis. If Mahan ruled today as he did a quarter of a century ago, the United States and Great Britain would plunge cheerfully into a new naval race convinced (as the dominant elements in Japan seem still to be convinced) that this was the natural destiny of peoples and the unquestionable imperative of national existence. It is quite possible, to be sure, that this is what will actually happen; but to large sections of opinion it will no longer appear as a normal and satisfactory outcome.

The true problem, therefore, does not lie in this or that specific naval policy of one or the other of the powers; rather is it to be found in the institution of navalism itself, as it is now generalized in all the powers concerned. Navalism must be examined as a single process, obeying its own laws, leading to its own consequences, in much the same way that one usually examines the phenomena of "capitalism" or "industrialism." Only in this way does it seem possible to bring any rational treatment at all to bear upon the naval issues which have now again arisen. From this point of view the objects of any one nation's policy can scarcely be more concrete than to avoid as far as may be the ultimate penalties which the navalist process appears to demand, while conserving as far as possible whatever real benefits it may seem to confer. And to the problem, when thus conceived, most of the actual statements of policy by the nations concerned become largely irrelevant. The formal declarations, for example, in which Mr. Norman H. Davis and Mr. Koki Hirota have enshrined their respective national policies are singularly unhelpful in the difficult questions here involved. Behind the deadlock which they have announced it is hard to find anything more satisfying than debater's briefs designed by each side to preserve a maximum of naval strength for itself while denying as much as possible to the other. In any attack upon the central question of navalism itself, one has to go much deeper than the documents.

In making such an attack, one may adopt either of two general avenues of approach. One may frankly challenge the basic assumptions upon which the navalist process rests, and seek to devise as substitutes for them some less dangerous and more viable foundations for national policy. Or one may recognize and accept these assumptions with an equal frankness, and then try to devise some method of applying them which will minimize their probable costs and yield more realistic benefits than those they have produced in the past. Both paths are hard.

THE MARXIST ARGUMENT

Of all approaches to the naval question, the intellectually simplest and least laborious is that of the Marxist, who merely declares that naval competition and imperialist war are the inevitable concomitants of Western industrial capitalism. It is useless, in this view, to look for any solution of the naval problem short of a complete reconstruction of world society upon a socialistic pattern. This represents a sweeping challenge to all the assumptions involved. If it calls for a minimum of precise analysis, it also represents the most far-reaching attack; and it is always possible, of course, that the Marxist may turn out in the end to have been right.

Unfortunately, his solution is impracticable for any immediate purpose. Nor does it seem necessary as yet to accept it as the only possible one. If our present economic and social order appears to favor competitive armaments and war in many ways, it has also provided a wealth of experience to suggest that neither is really essential to its continued functioning. The development of new historical rationalizations which, while remaining within the framework of the "capitalist system," would still exclude imperialist war and much of the apparatus of navalism, is perhaps not too much to hope for. In the immediate aftermath of the World War, as has been said, the attempt to construct such new rationalizations proved a failure. Under the strains of the depression, however, there have been a number of renewed beginnings in this direction; and some students—particularly Charles A. Beard—have sought to apply them directly to the naval problem.

BEARD'S VIEW: DOES NAVALISM PROMOTE NATIONAL INTEREST?

The essence of the Beard view is a denial of most of the primary assumptions of the sea power theory of history. It challenges the loose conceptions of "national interest" which have governed in the past; it seeks to introduce into the whole field of foreign policy a more adequate method of genuinely national accounting, and to free the conduct of foreign affairs from subservience to special rather than general interests. In so doing it rejects the necessity for naval prestige, for asserting a general "command of the sea," for the military acquisition of foreign markets, the forcible protection of American interests abroad and the military defense of American trade routes. It is thus able to reduce the function of an American Navy solely to the defense of the continental United States and the Panama Canal from invasion. A fleet operating defensively in its own waters enjoys today so great an advantage over an attacking fleet dispatched from distant bases that the precise parities and ratios of the treaty system would cease to be of much consequence to an American Navy confined to this function. Our naval establishment would still have to be related to those maintained elsewhere, but a few cruisers one way or the other would not make a great deal of difference, and in this way our naval policy would be freed from the narrow competitive standards of the treaty system.

Both the economic and the strategic position of the United States are peculiarly favorable to this approach. We are, of course, more nearly self-contained economically than any other great power, with the possible exception of the Soviet Union. The American Navy is not now and probably never has been in recent times equal to the defense of the home territory against simultaneous attack delivered across both oceans; but if we are willing to reject that possibility, we could regard other contingencies with equanimity as long as home defense were the only military objective. Naturally, we would at the same time have to resign policies which are maintainable only with an aggressive naval establishment. We would have to abandon any idea of forcibly controlling Japanese policy in the Far East or of defending the independence of the Philippines by other than peaceful means. The benefits now derived from these pretensions, if there are any, would have to be sought in other ways.

This is an extremely attractive solution. It could not give a final answer to the basic problem of navalism until the new attitude had been sincerely adopted by the other naval powers; but the American situation makes it easier for us than for either Great Britain or Japan to take the lead in experimenting with it. If we did so it would undercut, abroad as well as at home, many of the most important bases of naval expansion and might well alter the whole shape of the naval question. We could afford, in short, to set an example which might be followed elsewhere and which, if it were not, would probably cost us very little. At the same time it is useless to deny the immense practical difficulties which must be overcome before such a policy can be effectively adopted in this country. It necessitates the revision of countless long-established ideas and attitudes against the determined opposition of important vested interests and many sincere and earnest patriots. As yet hardly more than a beginning has been made upon the fundamental criticism of the accepted bases of national action and foreign policy for which it calls. We have only the foundations for a new rationalization; the task of working out the probable political and economic consequences, both short-term and long-term, to which it might lead is still to be done, and beyond that there remains the task of inculcating it in the public mind as a guiding principle of policy. Until the revision of popular attitudes is thoroughgoing and complete, any attempt to meet the Pacific question in this way would be more likely to end in a disastrous confusion than in success.

A NEW RATIO AT PARITY

A less fundamental mode of attack upon the problem is found in the suggestion that the United States should simply admit the Japanese demand for "parity" and so continue the ratio system on an equal basis. This proposal really lies halfway between the basic criticism of the navalist assumptions and the outright acceptance and application of them. It amounts to making the same kind of compromise with Japanese navalism which Great Britain made in 1922 with American navalism. It grants the reality and importance of sea power, but still further renounces the aim of complete command of the sea as impractical of attainment. Again, as in 1922, it would be accompanied by political settlements—the neutralization of the Philippines, for example, and further recognition and definition of Japanese "rights" in North China. As to the ethics of such an adjustment one makes no comment; but psychologically it should be a far more stable arrangement than that of 1922. Any international agreement which assumes the permanent inferiority of one party possesses an obvious weakness which does not attach to an agreement based on equality. "Parity" is a word of great power in the minds of peoples; and a Pacific settlement frankly based on parity all around might succeed in restraining the explosive force of the navalist philosophy where the Washington settlement failed. Nor would it very greatly alter the existing position. Despite the American claim to a naval strength adequate to fighting Japan in the Western Pacific, such a prospect is most unattractive even with a 5-3 predominance. The United States has actually shown no desire as yet forcibly to restrain Japanese aggression on the Asiatic continent; and it is evident enough that the practical diplomacy of the Far East today is based upon the fact of Japanese mastery there, whatever the paper claims of British and American policy may pretend.

The difficulty of this approach, however, lies in the fact that it first endorses the established assumptions of sea power and then demands their violation in practice. Outwardly, it would seem to yield about the same result as that described above under what has been called the Beard view. In both cases there would be three more or less equal navies; in both cases American interests in the Western Pacific would be beyond military safeguard, and consequently their protection would have to depend in the last analysis upon Japanese forbearance. The important difference is that the first view deliberately and consciously accepts this situation, denies the importance of the interests and resigns any idea of protecting them. The second view, however, while it would divest the United States of the military power to defend the interests, begins by insisting upon their reality and their value to the United States.

Such a policy might not be always or necessarily so illogical as it sounds. Five or six years ago an astute and far-seeing American statesmanship might have perceived that the course upon which the

United States was embarked in the Far East was not a permanently practicable one. It might have observed that we were committed at the time to a truculent assertion of American "rights" in that area, but were unwilling to accept the costs and risks of providing ourselves with the military power necessary to enforce these rights against the armed and ambitious state which occupied the ground. Such a statesmanship might have faced the decision (not unlike that which the British made when they negotiated the Anglo-Japanese Alliance in 1902) between entrusting these rights to a partnership with the new power or frankly preparing to defend them against it. As a matter of historical experience, international rights are actually preserved much more often and more surely by the voluntary engagements of those capable of violating them than they are by war. Had the first course been chosen, we might have entered into a partnership with Japan on mutually satisfactory terms. A neutralization of the Philippines and guarantees of our commercial rights on the Asiatic mainland might have been balanced against an understanding as to Japanese action in Manchuria and North China. Since it would have been a free bargain it would also have been a reliable one; and it is not impossible that both our interests in the Western Pacific and the international peace might have been safeguarded far more certainly than by any other method.

Now, unfortunately, the time has gone by. To attempt such a settlement now would be to put the United States too much in the position of the man who finally comes forward with an offer to sell his horse after it has already been annexed by the other party. It would create a situation resembling that detectable at times in the European disarmament negotiations, in which the French and British have been trying to enchain the Germans in a limitation treaty by progressively offering them just a little less rearmament than the Germans are progressively acquiring on their own account. This effort on the part of the French and British has not proved successful. For the same psychological reasons a similar effort by the United States in the Pacific is unlikely to succeed now, even if American public opinion should permit it to be made. As a matter of practical politics, it involves giving the Japanese everything which they are now asking, and for which they are offering absolutely nothing in return. Never to give a diplomatic adversary what he asks without exacting a *quid pro quo* is one of the cardinal principles of established nationalist diplomacy. One may question its wisdom in all cases—especially after the disaster of the World War, which was one of its perfect products—but for a state operating on the navalist-imperialist assumptions it is a principle which can hardly be disregarded. A bargain in which one party feels that he has compelled the other to yield everything is seldom of a lasting value; while there can be no doubt as to the furious popular resistance which any proposal of the kind would arouse in the United States. The idea involves the special difficulty that whereas Japan promptly exercised all her rights under the naval treaties, the United States has only now begun to do so. As a result the American Navy will, through the operation of building programs now under way, be progressively increasing its strength relative to the Japanese during the next two or three years. Here is an "advantage" of a sort extremely difficult for statesmanship in any country to surrender. We did give up a similar one to the British in 1922; but we got in return a formal abandonment of the classic "two power standard." We also got an immediate reduction in our proposed naval expenditure, and in 1922 naval expenditure seemed a more onerous matter than it does now in the high tide of deficit-budgeting and public works employment programs.

"COLLECTIVE SECURITY" IN THE PACIFIC

There remains the final approach to the problem—a frank acceptance of the navalist assumptions in so far as the United States and Japan are concerned, and an attempt to apply them with a little more foresight and consistency than have distinguished American policy in the past. This means deliberately entrusting peace in the Pacific to an effective naval predominance over Japan. The proposal to base Far Eastern stability upon a "collective system" seems, when it is carefully examined, to fall within this category, despite its appearance of substituting something other than the customary sanctions of force. In the absence of any of the compromises or re-orientations suggested above, a Far Eastern "collective system" can hardly mean more than an effective Anglo-American alliance for the restraint of Japan, just as the "collective system" in Europe has actually worked (in so far as it has worked at all) as an alliance of the *status quo* powers in restraint of the revisionists. If, however, the United States feels that it must play the traditional rôle of a navalist-imperial power in the Pacific, a reliable understanding of some sort with Great Britain would seem to be a first object of intelligent diplomacy.

The combination of the two greatest navies would represent a force which Japan could not possibly afford to challenge. Doubtless this would not alone halt the growth of Japanese navalism or the corresponding expansion of British and American navalisms—since all navalisms appear to grow quite as much through the operation of domestic as of foreign factors—but it might greatly lessen the chances of a war resulting. If in the Pacific it should be understood that the British and American Navies would always "shoot the same language" (as Walter Hines Page, in one of his visions of a *pax Anglo-Americana,* once put it) the effect might be a genuinely stabilizing one over a very considerable period of years. As to the remoter futures one might still entertain doubts. Yet it is difficult to deny that the overwhelming military preponderance of the French Army and its allies has actually served as a peace-keeping force in Europe since the World War. The bitter fruits of that method of keeping the peace are only now beginning to ripen. The solution may not be a safe one over a long term; the Pacific, however, presents a rather simpler problem in many ways than does contemporary Europe, and the Anglo-American understanding might suffice for as long into the future as anyone can now hope to see. A Japanese might argue that Pacific peace and stability could be based upon an Anglo-Japanese alliance in restraint of the United States quite as successfully as upon Anglo-American alliance in restraint of Japan. It is scarcely appropriate for an American to pass judgment on the point; although he may suggest that a wholly neutral observer might find reasons of consanguinity, common cultures, complementary national interests and so on, to indicate that the Anglo-American solution would on the whole be the more practicable. Since the viability of any such solution, moreover, is in direct proportion to the *disparity* of force which it gives, it is desirable to get the strongest powers in the one camp and confine the weaker to the other. The arrangement is of course an inherently brutal one, and again ethics must be left out of the question.

Unhappily, the construction of such an alliance—or understanding, or "collective system," or "security pact"—is itself a matter of no little delicacy and uncertainty. There are elements in Great Britain—particularly influential in naval matters—which regard alliance with the United States with no great enthusiasm. British diplomatists are quite conscious of the value to them of the balance of power, which they have so far managed to retain. In the course of the 1934 London naval talks, the competition between the Japanese and American delegations, each to secure British support against the other, was almost painfully apparent. Here the Americans had on their side the influence of the British Dominions, which have been consistently suspicious and fearful of Japanese purposes since the war, and memories of the Anglo-Japanese Alliance of 1902, which failed to give the British the secure safeguard to their Far Eastern affairs upon which they had counted. In the end the Americans appear to have won at least a negative victory at London, in that the Japanese effort to drive a wedge between us and Great Britain was an obvious failure. The British, at the same time, appear to have avoided any positive commitments to the United States with great skill, and it is reasonable to suppose that Great Britain will prove extremely reluctant to identify herself as definitely hostile to Japan.

The American public, on the other hand, has never been trained to the difficult, uncertain and forbidding business of alliance-making. It has always greatly preferred to eat its cake and have it too. American policy has never faced the question of defining the proper relationship between the United States and Great Britain, and in the result we have followed a course so vacillating and irresponsible as to make the British very wary of putting their foreign policy at the mercy of our own. When we were adopting our great naval program in 1916, some of its proponents were careful to explain that we might disregard British naval strength in calculating our requirements, as there was no possibility of menace from that quarter. Yet two or three years later, when it appeared that the program might actually give us predominance over Great Britain, that fact became an argument for completing it, and many felt that our grant of "parity" in 1922 was a shameful and dangerous surrender. The grant of "parity" having been made, however, Anglo-American naval cooperation became the only logical basis of future policy; it was but five years later, nevertheless, that the Geneva conference was broken up by a not very significant squabble between American and British naval men seeking to gain a relative advantage over each other. In 1927 the Japanese were all but forgotten; yet now, in another seven years, it is suddenly the Japanese who are the menace, and there is but the slightest American interest in the strength of the British Navy, except that Americans would be glad to see it strong to assist us against Japan.

Such waverings point to the difficulties, from the American side no less than from the British, in the way of any really firm Anglo-American understanding in the Pacific. Under the vague sort of loose cooperation which is likely to be the most that is practicably attainable, each power will almost inevitably maneuver to derive all the advantages of an alliance while trying to make sure that any penalties it may involve in the way of actual fighting will fall solely upon the other. The dangers inherent in such a situation are too obvious for comment. The world has had a great deal of recent experience with imprecise "understandings" which end by commiting each partner much farther than it realized and costing it much more than it had anticipated. If the danger is clearly recognized, a careful statesmanship may be competent to avert it; but it remains as an argument against the adequacy of any solution based upon military cooperation between the United States and Great Britain.

A NEW NAVAL RACE

If one excludes the Anglo-American alliance, however, there seems to be nothing left, under the basic navalist assumptions, save to plunge into a frank American-Japanese naval race and hope for the best. This alternative again presents a difficult task for the prophet. The dangers are sufficiently apparent. It is scarcely a practicable undertaking for the United States alone to create and maintain a navy great enough to fight Japan in the Western Pacific with any certainty of quick success. The independent naval race would therefore have nothing like the stabilizing effect of the overwhelming Anglo-American alliance. It would, on the other hand, make American naval power an immediate and important element in every Japanese calculation, and so would tend to limit adventures that might otherwise be undertaken. It would at the same time leave the United States still committed to objectives which would be affected by such adventures and which we would not have the military force certainly to defend. That is a situation sufficiently likely to be productive of dangerous "incidents," while the naval race itself would be a prolific source of them. The amount of fear, animosity and inflammatory statement already generated by the attempt simply to avert a race is a vivid indication of what might be expected with directly competitive programs being laid down year by year, with the navalists of each power exaggerating the menace presented by the other, with the press of both ringing to cries of "Two keels for one!" and the like.

The most ominous aspect of such a competition lies in the fact that Japan is fundamentally the much weaker power, though for the moment she holds a strong position. The pressure upon her statesmen to defend that position while there was yet time would be a powerful one. It is to be suspected that the consciousness of ultimate weakness is a far more potent cause of modern war between major powers than is the pride of strength. It seems not impossible that only a few years of active and direct naval competition would suffice to create a situation like that which led the Japanese to attack Russia in 1904 or drove the Austro-Hungarian statesmen to strike their savage blow at the rising Russo-Serb power in the Balkans in 1914.

As against such a catastrophe, the only direct hope held out by the navalist philosophy is the hope that the financial exhaustion of one side or the other will lead to its quiet withdrawal from an unprofitable competition, with a gradual tranquilization of the whole area. Japanese naval spokesmen have been proclaiming this hope recently with a great confidence and a considerable arrogance. Captain Tamon Yamaguchi, for example, the naval attaché of the Japanese Embassy at Washington, has publicly announced that no American statesman could justify an extended naval race "to the people, who are after all almost breaking under the terrific strain of the nation's financial burden." To an American it is obvious that such pronouncements are the best possible means of guaranteeing that the United States will keep up the race to the end. Unfortunately, although American spokesmen are rather more cautious in their public utterances, it must be plain to the Japanese that an identical hope represents the sole practical end envisioned by the present policy of the United States. The whole American attitude clearly implies the expectation that if the United States only puts up a strong enough show of determination, the Japanese will soon quit, and that calm—more or less upon the Washington terms— will be restored. This can only spur the Japanese to a firmer resolve not to quit.

For if the expectation tends to defeat itself when held by the Japanese, it must equally tend to do so when held by the United States. It is true that certain other factors can be cited in favor of the view that Japan will sooner or later tacitly abandon her effort and resign herself to the old position. The threat of joint Anglo-American action against her may seem too great. She is already assuming commitments on the Asiatic mainland too large to permit her to risk a naval war. She is at the moment going through a reorganization of her domestic political and social structure; the necessities of domestic rivalry have directly exacerbated her foreign policy, and when the reorganization is complete she may adopt a less truculent attitude toward the world. Finally, she is much nearer the end of her financial tether, if there is such a thing, than the United States.

It is to be noted that Japanese naval men themselves, while insisting with complete intransigeance upon the principle of naval equality, have as yet brought forth no programs for attaining it in practice. They apparently do not now propose to challenge American superiority in battleship strength, and there is considerable obscurity as to just what they expect to build in the lighter categories when they have recovered their freedom of action. Their present objective apparently is to make their position in the Western Pacific impregnable to attack, whether from Vladivostok, Singapore or the American Pacific bases, rather than to equip themselves for offensive operations beyond that area. Under the circumstances, it may be that they will actually lay down no tonnage which the United States will not either be willing to disregard (as in the case of their new 500-ton, non-treaty torpedo boats) or else be able to match without too much difficulty on the 5-3 formula. It is possible, in other words, that juridical equality will prove sufficient; that the disappearance of the treaty will reconcile both nations (and their navalists) to its essential provisions; and that actual construction in the future will proceed more or less as in the past, on an effective 5-3 basis but without the unsettling psychology of an embittered naval race.

All these arguments have been advanced; some of them may have weight, but none is too convincing in the light of experience elsewhere, and it would certainly be rash to count on them. To hope for peaceful continuance of treaty ratio building is to overlook the fears and rivalries which the respective navalisms would have to engender in their own peoples to sustain what would, after all, be a very considerable naval effort. It would seem to be particularly rash to count on the financial argument alone, at a time when most of the principal industrial powers seem to be desperately searching for ways not to save but to spend more money in the effort to keep their economies going. Nor is it easy to think of an instance, save, perhaps, that of the Washington Treaty, in which a power has deliberately resigned an active armament race with another because it could not afford it. Even to attempt a prediction as to the scale upon which Japan may be able to sustain competitive building against the United States would first require a prediction as to the course and outcome of the depression and exhaustive analysis of its effect upon the public finances of all the powers concerned. The end of such an inquiry would be a morass of guess-work and uncertainty. The possibility remains that Japan may resign; but it is a possibility which offers a most unsatisfactory basis for national policy.

The uncertainty deepens if one attempts to include the possible intervention of factors which have not been considered here. Either a Russo-Japanese war or a war in Europe would alter the entire face of the problem in ways totally beyond prediction. The same may perhaps be said as to the intervention of new technical factors—the development of new ship types, new weapons, or new tactical methods. The submarine and aviation together have already made it far more difficult to protect one's trade routes; they have also greatly enhanced the defensive power of a battle fleet operating near to its own shores. In this, however, they have merely exaggerated elements which were always a characteristic of naval war. Since both the submarine and the airplane are still relatively short-range weapons and the Pacific is an immense ocean, they have probably not yet effected any profound change in the general strategy. Already, however, airplanes are being built capable of carrying quite formidable loads across the longest distances which divide the islands lying between the United States and Japan. Anything like a mass air attack across the Pacific still seems to lie in a fairly remote future, but one cannot neglect the possibility that aviation—or some other technical development—may materially alter the purely military aspects of the question.

The frank American-Japanese naval race thus presents a future clouded at best by the ominous and the unpredictable. Perhaps the most hopeful aspect here is the fact that the fighting of any Pacific war at all now presents to both admiralties a strategic problem of the utmost difficulty. In midsummer of 1914 the various governments had only to post their mobilization orders—as they might have touched a button—and a war carefully planned and prepared for over many years was instantly in full and bloody career. A naval conflict in the Pacific could not be so easily joined. For the United States it must always mean a tremendous and exhausting effort for the slightest of gains; for Japan it must mean accepting the risk of disastrous, and ultimately very probable, defeat in the certainty that no vital injury could be inflicted upon the United States. If the Japanese seriously regard us as a menace to their safety, they must also admit that it is beyond their power to remove the menace by war. Even in the Russo-Japanese War they failed permanently to free themselves from the Russian threat; yet in that war they had to repulse merely a spearhead thrust out across one of the longest and least serviceable lines of communication in modern military history. With the United States it would be a harder problem.

It is thus not impossible, perhaps, that a Pacific naval race might run on indefinitely, leading to no particular explosion and being diverted or abandoned in the end because of changes, not now foreseeable, in the many other factors which determine the final course of human history. It is not impossible—but one can hardly say more. In accepting an American-Japanese naval race as the appropriate answer to the naval problem of the Pacific, one must also accept the fact that it means embarking upon a policy unquestionably filled with a war danger and leading to ends which cannot be predicted.

VI

IS THE TIME RIPE FOR A
NEW THEORY OF NAVALISM?

THE collapse of the treaty system presents to all three major naval powers a serious problem in fundamental national policy. The several lines along which it seems that solutions might be constructed have been examined above, and an attempt made to assess the inherent limitations and potentialities of each. In an ideal world each power would make some such analysis as this; it would weigh the resultant alternatives, adopt that which seemed most hopeful, accept its inevitable disadvantages and follow it with complete consistency in order to make sure of enjoying the corresponding advantages. Few things are more probable than that none of the powers will actually do this. Even states under so centralized a control as Japan appears to be are victims, in the real world, of half-measures, irresolutions, conflicting purposes and the eternal inability of peoples to understand that it is impossible to enjoy the best features of any given policy without likewise suffering its worst.

It may confidently be expected that the actual policies followed by all three powers will represent efforts to combine in greater or less proportion all the main types of solution. There will be attempts simultaneously to reject the navalist assumptions and to carry them to their conclusions. There will be attempts to yield to Japanese demands and to repress them, to challenge American naval power and to surrender before it, to gain the advantages of alliance and preserve the irresponsibilities of freedom. Because the true values involved, in terms of practical human welfare, are all so completely elusive, a certain atmosphere of unreality will cling about the whole proceeding; and it is hard to expect any outcome more satisfactory than a series of temporary expedients and adjustments. The possibility that among these expedients there may prove to be an actual war cannot be disregarded, but neither can it be calculated. It seems safe to say, however, that the navalist institution no longer admits of any final settlement—in the sense of a reasonably permanent and generally acceptable working adjustment. For that one must await the appearance of new rationalizations of history and international relations, adequate to confine this two-edged weapon of modern navalism within limits to which contemporary society can agree.

APPENDIX

THE Washington Treaty of 1922 was concluded for a ten-year period. It prescribed by name the capital ships (battleships and battle cruisers which each power might retain. It then specified certain adjustments which might be made at once to reduce the fleets thus authorized to a more equitable relationship (the chief of these were the completion of the Japanese *Mustu* and the construction by the British of the *Nelson* and *Rodney,* with corresponding retirements of older tonnage). Finally, it fixed the "replacement" capital ship strength, beyond which the powers might not thereafter build, at 525,000 tons for the United States and Great Britain, 315,000 tons for Japan and 175,000 tons for France and Italy.

Aircraft carrier strength was similarly limited to 135,000 tons for the United States and Great Britain, 81,000 tons for Japan and 60,000 tons for France and Italy. Great Britain and the United States agreed not to extend their naval bases and fortifications in the Western Pacific. At the same time the size and armament of individual ships thereafter laid down was limited to 35,000 tons and 16-inch rifles for battleships; 27,000 tons and 8-inch rifles for aircraft carriers; 10,000 tons and 8-inch rifles for cruisers.

The London Treaty of 1930 extended the capital ship and aircraft carrier limitations for a further five years, providing at the same time for the retirement of older battleships with no replacement, so that the British fleet of twenty vessels and the American fleet of eighteen were each reduced to fifteen ships and the Japanese fleet reduced from ten to nine. This part of the treaty was ratified by France and Italy; the remaining sections, referring to the lesser categories, were ratified only by the United States, Great Britain and Japan. Through a variety of agreements as to new building, scrapping, age limits and so on they provided that upon the expiration of the treaty on December 31, 1936 the auxiliary fleets of the three powers would not exceed the following figures:

	UNITED STATES		GREAT BRITAIN		JAPAN	
	No.	Tons	No.	Tons	No.	Tons
8-inch-gun cruisers	18	180,000	15	146,800	12	108,000
6-inch-gun cruisers		143,500		192,200		100,450
Destroyers		150,000		150,000		105,500
Submarines		52,700		52,700		52,700

To reach this position, however, required not only the building of much new tonnage but the scrapping, by all three powers, of considerable amounts of existing tonnage which, although technically "over age" before the final date, would still possess real military value. Very little of this tonnage has as yet been scrapped, nor is there any time-schedule in the treaty under which it must be retired. There is merely the vague provision that it is to be scrapped "gradually" prior to December 31, 1936. The treaty also provided that a conference be held in 1935 to consider the prolongation of the limitation system. There now seems no chance of holding such a conference, but that makes it only the more essential that a conference be held to regularize this matter of scrapping within the remaining life of the treaty, and so eliminate an obvious source of dangerous misunderstanding.